THE MAKING
OF A
DIAMOND

My Personal Journey

Hope T. Melton

ZYIA CONSULTING
Illuminate & Transcend

The Making of A Diamond: My Personal Journey

To contact the author about speaking at your event email
hopemeltonministries@gmail.com

ZYIA CONSULTING
Illuminate & Transcend

Zyia Consulting
Book Writing & Publishing Company
www.nyishaddavis.com
nyisha.d.davis@gmail.com
678-881-5983

Unless otherwise noted, all Scripture quotations are taken from the www.blueletterbible.org.

ISBN: 9798592681677

Printed in the United States of America.

Dedication

To my beloved sister, Sherae E. RIvers. Though she is no longer here I am thankful for all the love and impartation that impacted my life forever. Her legacy lives on. I am so honored to have had the opportunity to have had tHis Jewel as my sister. Never forget.

Portia Phillips, I will forever hold the memories of her in my heart.
Never forget you, sis!

Acknowledgment

First, I thank the Holy Spirit who is the teacher of all things.

I would like to acknowledge my mother who has been a great example of faith and motherhood; always being there in the good times and challenging times never gave up on me. Love you, Mama.

I acknowledge my brother, Charles Porter, a true older brother. Love you.

I acknowledge my close Family and Beloved friends.
Thanks for all the support and love.

I would like to acknowledge Apostle Patrick J. Brown of the Renewal Center, for helping me in understanding my scribal anointing, Apostles Clyde and Scheherazade Daniels of Dominion Harvest Network for teaching the Kingdom of God through demonstration, Pastor Tracy Holley of New life Fellowship; thank you for always holding me down, Pastor Laura Price who has been a great example of faith in action, Elder Lynda Axson who has been a witness to the miracle of God in my life made manifest, Nyisha D. Davis (Zyia Consulting: Book Writing & Publishing Company), thank you for being apart of me birthing this book and Prophetess LaShanda Jones for the opportunity to be a co-author of "Reloaded and Dangerous" (shout out to all the Bombshells and Ambassadors).

I also like to thank all the leaders through the years that have impacted my life on various levels, forever thankful.

Foreward

Today, more than ever there is a need to understand our individual worth and value. This understanding is not defined by our modern traditions or our societal cultural norms. Our worth and values are define by God; who created us. In order for us to embrace who God created us to be, there is a process through which we must undergo in order for us to become all that He has destined us to be. We must understand that God takes us through a transformative process of growth and development.

In this book, Prophet Hope shares her personal journey of her transformation process from becoming a Diamond in the rough to becoming a Diamond out of the rough. She shares that during her process to becoming a Diamond, She had to endure intense pressure, so that a beautiful polished Diamond with clarity and weight can display reflecting the true value of what she carries. I can personally attest to her transformation process by which she has allowed the power of God to produce an unshakable faith which is the bedrock of her transformation.

Although the testimonies shared in this book are about Prophet Hope's journey, my prayer for you as you read you will reflect, pray, and put into action the principles that are demonstrated in this book. "The Making of a Diamond" can change your life as you allow God to bring you to an eye opening experience that will cause you to identify the Diamond on the inside of you. I admonish you to recognize your past, move past it and allow God to bring you into your pre-destined purpose.

Dr. Scheherazade Daniels
Apostle and Cofounder,
Dominion Harvest Ministries
Dominion Ambassadors Network
Atlanta, Georgia

Foreword

All moments in our lives are key moments. Moments to understand who we are and why we are created to be and become. Some may ask the reflective question, "what am I becoming?" In <u>The Making of a Diamond</u>, Hope Melton not only poses that question rhetorically, she answers by sharing her journey and pathway to realizing who she is and the actions taken to get to that place of recognizing that identity.

Using the typology of geology, Hope documents her journey like the formation of a diamond, a precious jewel used as an analogy of the treasure that is found in earthen vessels. She suggests that the diamond is the divine deposit that is buried with each human being. As in nature, the formation of natural diamonds requires very high temperatures and pressures from conditions under the surface of the earth. Diamonds are then formed and stored in these "diamond stability zones" and come to the surface during deep-source eruptions.

Hope shares from her journey of discovery and excavation that buried within each of us, there will be conditions that form greatness within that was formed in the image and likeness of God. Yet, through moments of internal pressure, the temperature of our attitudes and the eruptions in our souls, the emerging diamond process unfolds.

In nature and from the naked eye, we can't see the formation diamond crystals because it is too deep to dig or see, but we can see its results. Hope shares in life there is intense pressure in diamond formation. The weight of the overlying rock bearing down, so that combination of high temperature and high pressure is what's necessary to grow the diamond, but that process does not take away from the diamond, it only adds to the glory to be revealed. Let this book encourage you in the making of you.

Patrick J. Brown, M.A.

Executive Director, Renewal Culture & Context

The Renewal Center

Author of Change Matters: 21 Principles of the Process, Purpose and Product of Change

CONTENT

INTRODUCTION

"The word Diamond derives from the Greek word "Adamas," which means invincible or indestructible." I invite you to go with me as I share transparent, profound moments in my life's journey. This is how I became a Diamond out of the rough my trials and triumphs struggles and how I overcame. My moments of cutting, breaking, and shaping me into the Diamond I have developed into.

The importance of this book is to uplift, encourage, and edify you in your Diamond journey. It will help you truly understand and know your value so you can overcome everything that has tried to stand in your way. Through all the pain and struggle, through every dark moment that you have faced, I want to share with you that you can and will arise from being a Diamond in the rough to a Diamond out of the rough. You can make it; just beyond the darkness is the beautiful light.

I will share with you principles to enhance and help you get a better understanding of your value. As I applied these principles to my life the Diamond in me began to develop and shine bright.

Chapter 1

THE ROUGH

Psalms 139:14 KJV

I will praise thee; for I am fearfully [and] wonderfully made: marvellous [are] thy works; and [that] my soul knoweth right well.

Welcome to my rough place. I was the Diamond which was buried and hidden; a Diamond in the rough. So much to say about my beginning. Where should I start? Where do I begin? I'll start at the precious time of my teenage years.

Diamonds Formed

"Diamonds were formed over 3 billion years ago deep within the Earth's crust under conditions of intense heat and pressure that" cause carbon atoms to crystallize forming Diamonds."

At this time, I did not even realize that I had any value. I sure did not understand the value of a Diamond and how it related to me. I was totally lost even though I was raised in the church. By the time I reached my tender teenage years, I was already set to a road of destruction. Despite growing up in a home with a Godly mother, where I received love and attention, I was already broken and began to make poor decisions that would affect my life for many years to come. I was troubled by rejection, hurt by issues with my father which led to many different feelings that I hid and held in.

When you do not understand and know your value, it does not matter who or what people tell you are, you will not get the revelation. The Diamond, in its rarity and beauty, is a symbol of purity and innocence, of love and fidelity, and embraces strength of character, ethics, and faithfulness to oneself and others. It is indicative of the loving and open nature with which one came into the physical realm and encourages the aspect of truth and trust.

Being I was broken, I could not embrace who God had created me to be. I had no true understanding of the worth and value of myself. I thought that if I would give those around me what they wanted in return I would get what I so deeply desired; to be loved and accepted. The purity of who God had created me to be was lost. In moments of despair, I just had to close my eyes and take a moment to breathe. At times the process just seemed like such a heavy burden to bare.

I had lost all hope and vision for my dreams. I detached myself from education, school, and all the things I was supposed to be enjoying as a teenager. I was already starting to deal with the heaviness of life. Connecting to others who were lost and not understanding or knowing their value just made things more complex.

Now, I was connected to bad habits, things, and bad relationships. There was a lot of enabling one another's bad decisions and poor behavior. All that I had been taught I threw away not realizing those things were the things that established a good foundation.

I threw it all away for an easy way out to escape the hurt, pain, and disappointments I experience as a child up until my teenage years. I wanted to escape the reality of what I was dealing with on the inside. I was crying out from within. I hid this from everyone and anyone close to me.

At the age of thirteen years, I experienced a major rejection from my Dad. In a courtroom full of people, he stated that he was not sure if I were his daughter. From that moment, my world went into a major downward spiral. My mom and I separated from living with my Dad. Now, here I am having to adjust to this new life and great transition.

Although I still had a relationship with my dad, it was not quite the same anymore. From this downward spiral, I began to get involved in sex, violence, gangs, and cutting class on a regular. I was drinking and smoking weed as well which began to develop very bad dependencies. I was a Diamond in the rough and I was buried deep where I had lost all my shine and my luster. I felt devalued rejection and hopeless. Oh, the pain ran deep and I had no idea how deep until it

would be time to do the cutting.

If anyone was going to find me, they would have to dig deep. Little did I know that God was going to uproot me out of this dark place. Where my road was set to destruction. After an in-depth reading and understanding of a Diamond, I realize that every step is necessary for its development. Every step of my personal process was needed in the development during this journey. I admit I was up against a wall.

I felt like quitting and many times I just wanted to give up because I could not see my way out. I continue to press and move forward, knowing that the pressure was bringing me to my place of much time and effort were given to finding Diamonds. My question was, will anyone take the time and effort with me? I soon understood that God was was healing me and I was being set free. My mind was made up and I wanted to be free.

There were so many rough edges that had to be removed. I tell you, I spent many days in self-reflection and crying. I did not know if the road would get any better. Or if I had to just live forever with the decisions I had made that affected my life. I was a piece of coal under pressure. The pressure brought me face to face with who I had become. It brought me to the accountability for my own actions; not blaming others for the decision that I made. Of course, things that happen to us are not all our fault. I had to be able to discern what I had done, what I had allowed it to be done to me, and those things I had no control over were not my fault.

When you are in a place of despair, you feel alone hopeless, or even in a dark place. God saved me. He encourages you on your journey to know that there is still hope in any situation that seems dead and hopeless. God will use it for His glory.

PRAYER

Dear God,

    I thank you for every life experience, whether good or bad. I thank you that through these times it has helped me to grow and appreciate the life you have given me. Help me to make my transition from my rough place to the ordained place you have for me so that every aspect of my journey will bring edification and encouragement to the lives of others. Help me to let go of trauma, hurt, unforgiveness, low-esteem, all bad thoughts, and shame from my past. I embrace the new me and all you have called me to be. Amen.

I like you to just take a moment to reflect on the prayer and think about or even write down your feelings regarding your rough places. Not from the standpoint of a victim but from a place of being victorious and more than an overcomer.

PRINCIPLES FOR THE PROCESS

- ❖ If you have not, establish a relationship with God.
- ❖ Pray while you are coming out of the rough or even if you are still in the rough.
- ❖ Learn to let go of the past; maybe a series of bad decisions or bad things that have happened.
- ❖ Let unhealthy things and people go.
- ❖ It's okay to reach out for help; counseling, grief recovery, and/ or spiritual leadership.
- ❖ Have a support system; family and/or friend(s).

Be in touch with how you feel: moments of sadness, anger, disappointment, depression, hopelessness, guilt, and/or shame. These take time to overcome. Take the time that is needed to do so. There is no rush. You want to process your feelings so that you can be healed and made whole.

Ephesians 2:5

Even when we were dead in sins, hath quickened us together

with Christ, (by grace ye are saved;)

Chapter 2

THE PROCESS

John 15:2

Every branch in me that beareth not fruit he taketh away: and every branch that

beareth fruit, he purgeth it,

that it may bring forth more fruit.

Diamond cutting is the practice of shaping a diamond from a rough stone into a faceted gem. Cutting Diamond requires specialized knowledge, tools, equipment, and techniques because of its extreme difficulty.

Welcome to my process; my cutting, and my difficult and most challenging journey. After many years of heartache, defeat, let downs, betrayal, pain, and rejection. I had grown to a place where I had become tired. My life was in shambles. All the dreams I had for my life had become a nightmare. The cutting was so deep because a lot of issues were deeply rooted within me. The cuts were brutal at times. But were necessary for my freedom and development of being shaped into a Diamond.

Yet, I still had no way of knowing how or when I would ever escape this madness that I called life. Not to mention the failed relationships, bad decisions, and compromising that made me have or feel no self-worth at all. I was trapped and buried, crying out for help but no one could see or hear my cries.

I had become hopeless in my relationships with men. I was looking for them to fulfill something in me that only God could do. I was broken and in hopes, I would find someone to love and fix me. I had this dream of having a husband and kids but that reality was soon crushed due to poor decisions, a marriage that ended in divorce after failing. I had hoped if I give them what they want, they would in return give me what I wanted and needed; what I felt was missing.

But in the end, I went from relationship to relationship; being buried deeper and deeper. I had become an empty shell, just exciting. All my hope was gone. My faith was lacking and my foundation was crushed. Yet, I had this fake smile and demeanor on the outside that I was okay living from day to day.

At this point, I was an adult. Living from paycheck to paycheck, hustling to get by or make money. It did not matter, I was just trying to survive. But soon it began to get to a point where I became tired of the circus that I had created. I got tired of the failed relationships and betrayal from those who were supposed to be friends. Being in poverty and doing whatever it took to make a dollar. I realized that I had become something that I did not like. I knew something had to happen to free me from this place.

My depression began to get deeper and suicidal thoughts began to invade my mind. I had become cold and heartless because that was the way of the streets; the only way to survive. My wild ways took me into dark places I never that I would ever be a part of. I was tired sick and tired, my mind was sick, my life was sick, I was in a true 911 situation. Raised in church yet my heart was from God. No relationship God was absent from my life.

The Moments of Light

I watched my mom's relationship with God. She would try to call me in her room so that she could read the Bible to me. I just did not want to hear. I would see her in the morning when she would pray. I knew she was putting in prayers for me. By observing her intimacy with God, it gave me a sense of hope that maybe one day I would have a true relationship with God such as my mother. There were small moments like those, that in the midst of my darkness, I would see a glimpse of light. Yet, I was in a dark and cold place. I knew in my heart that it was God letting me know "I am here." Even at my darkest moments, it did not stop that glimpse of light that would break through form time to time.

I had got myself into some major trouble. My goodness, the pressure was very heavy. I thought, "How could things get any worse?" But it did. I was up against a wall and fighting for my survival. I knew things were not looking good and something had to happen, fast. I knew if I kept this up there would not be a good ending for me.

One day, my mom invited me to a church service. At first, I hesitated about going. Because at the time, I wanted nothing to do with the church after I saw the many things some churches were involved in. Sunday morning came and I decided I would just go ahead and get ready and accompany my mom to church.

We walked through those doors and my goodness I was nervous. But something began to happen when the choir began to sing. Something ignited that had not been since I was a child. As I sat next to my mom, tears began to fill my eyes but my pride would not let it show. I did not want my mom to see it.

After that Sunday, something for sure was taking place in my spirit. So, I decided to go back to their weekly Bible study without my mom. I was accompanied by my friend. Once they did the altar call, there was a tug in my heart, pulling on my spirit, and so I joined. I now rededicated my life back to Christ Not realizing that my life was going to change forever. It would change for the better

Now that I redirected my life back to Christ, some things began to change. I mean, I was still hanging out and doing the usual but after a while, I disconnected from certain friends' unhealthy relationships and certain places and I began to just leave all the drama behind. I started to disconnect and yet the whole while I did not miss a service at church.

1 Corinthians 2:14

But the natural man does not receive the things of the Spirit of God, for they are foolishness to him; nor can He know them, because they are spiritually discerned.

Crossroads

I was still indulging in a life of sin. Yet, I was feeling the tug of God to get right. My natural man wanted to stay in sin but my spiritual man was being awakened. I remember praying a prayer because I was tired, felt trapped, and I wanted to be free. I said, "God if you do not do something I am going to die. " It was my heart cry; a desperate cry that only God could hear.

I remember the church was having a conference and the cost was sixty dollars. I was standing in the rotunda part of the church, deciding if I was going to go. A lady walked up to me and said, "Are you going to come? It will be worth it." As I stood there, my mind was racing. I was thinking I could take this money, go get alcohol, weed, and a pill and just chill or I can spend this money on the church conference ticket. I was so desperate for a breakthrough I spent it on a ticket for the conference.

On the first night, there was an altar call. I ran to that altar in desperate need of a breakthrough from God. I wanted God to deliver my soul from the torment; to break free from the old life. I stood there with my hands lifted high, waiting for God to touch me. My heart beating every fast as the women of God walked down a crowded line of people. She began to get closer and I could feel the Spirit of God. At that time, I did not know what to call what I was feeling. All I knew is that I was feeling something powerful I had never felt before.

My eyes were closed and then I felt the touch of God through the women of God. I began to scream and shout. I was not sure what was happening. All I know is I could not control it. It was strange because I was so used to hiding and controlling my emotions. After my eyes open and I was unsure of my surroundings, I was facing another way and there were people gathered around me. I was confused a bit but I knew something had happened.

I felt lighter and it was like a huge burden had been lifted off me. I had been delivered and my soul was light and I felt free. As I went back to my seat, I felt like a new person. I had been revived from the dead. When I was at that alter, there had been a release as I shouted and cried very loudly. God had touched me and made me whole. But even after this great breakthrough, there was still a lengthy process that I had to face; deep-rooted issues that I had to be willing to allow to uproot some strongholds that need to be broken. Have you been in a place that you were so desperate. I was in that place. I had no fancy prayer. All I had was a cry from my heart.

"I was trapped and I wanted to be free. I said God if
you do not do something I am going to die. "

Diamond the Processing

"Before a Diamond is processed, a Diamond may look like a dull piece
of glass. There are several different Diamond processing
methods used."

My life had changed and the process was just beginning. I called up a few of my girls and told them I was not going to clubs or bars, not smoking or getting drunk anymore. They all thought something was wrong with me. they thought that after a while I would change my mind. But I did not and soon they realized that I was very serious. They could not know or understand the position that my mind and spirit were in.

God found me and I began to hear from Holy Spirit often but there God began to, I was filled with the Holy Spirit and on fire for God. Yet, there were some things I had to face. A part of the process was the renewing of my thinking. But I had to go through the process. Many things had to be changed and my relationship with God had to be built up. A relationship not based upon religious formalities

There were many stages of my process I had to start from the bottom. My process came with some real truths I had to face and deal with; a lot of corrupt and unhealthy behaviors. I had to face myself. I had to deal with the disappointments most of which I had caused. I had to learn to forgive myself, even before I started to forgive others. In my process, I had to embrace myself. It was rocky, in the beginning, but as time went on I began to process what had happened to me with my life.

How did I get to this place? How was I going to get out? Accepting Christ back into my life was just the first step but the cutting was real. The hurt was real the pain and rejection were real. Have you been at a place you just do not know how you arrived at that point? Not only did I let myself down but I had to process that I let those who loved me down. Some would say I was a hopeless case but God deemed it otherwise. I was coming face to face looking in the mirror and knowing that there was a greater purpose for me but, the process could not be avoided.

I had to look at the root cause of my situation so that I could go through my process with truth and not blindfolded to it. Enough was enough. I was also facing the things that I had submerged within some things in my mind. The torment of the things I told myself and the things that were told and said to me. I was in the real process of healing and it started with my mind. How I processed life and all that I had been through. I had not, until this time, truly dealt with them. Yet, this process was necessary for me to emerge into the Diamond I was supposed to be.

Diamond Polishing

"The Diamond's finish consists of 2 important attributes: Polish & Symmetry. A Diamond's Polish is determined by the manufacturing process of a Diamond. Typically, after the Diamond is cut and faceted, it is polished to bring out the shine and smooth finish of the Diamond. Polish can affect the Diamond's sparkle if not done well. It is a secondary characteristic of the Diamond's cut grade that will sometimes, not always impact the assigned cut grade."

Through my process, I realize there are a lot of things that I must face in order for me to truly evolve. I had to face the process head-on. No more excuses, procrastination, or blaming others. It was up to me to endure this process. This was one of the hardest parts because I had to also be okay with being cut so that I could shine bright like a Diamond.

Though I am continually being processed each day, I aim to become the version of me that God had predestined for me. Many layers have been ripped off and much has been uprooted. My life was being changed and my mind was renewed all during the process. I encourage you today to own and embrace your process. Your process may not be like mine but we all have to go through this. May you press on and God strengthens you during your time of being processed as a Diamond.

PRAYER

God,

    I thank you for my process. Help me to embrace my process as it modes shapes and helps me to move into my purpose. Help me not to become bitter or lose hope and faith during the process. Give me the supernatural strength to press through. I know at times it may not be easy. Help me to lay all my burdens at Your feet. I thank you that all things will work together for my good. And that this process will bring me to a place of peace and appreciation. Amen.

Take a moment to reflect on your process, what have you learned, and what wisdom you have gained. Celebrate your victories and your overcoming moments.

PRINCIPLES FOR PROCESSING

- ❖ Don't hate your process. Embrace your process. It's all about development in your journey.
- ❖ Understand what you do and why you do it.
- ❖ Have a mature person that you can be accountable to.
- ❖ What has your process taught you? What can you take from it? How has it made you better?
- ❖ Take a moment to reflect on the steps you have taken.
- ❖ What actions will you take to ensure that you are moving towards your place of promise?
- ❖ Make necessary changes to fit the place where you are headed; a change in lifestyle, learning, and transformation of mind and thoughts.

Chapter 3

VALUE

Psalm 139:14

I will praise thee; for I am fearfully and wonderfully made: marvellous are thy works; and that my soul knoweth right well.

After going through one of the most tenacious processes of life, for this new place God has called me to, I needed to understand my value of who God created me to be. Not just some self vain talk of lifting myself. But one understanding the treasure that God had placed on the inside of me and learning to walk this out. How I am valuable to God. and breaking away from what the world considers a definition of value.

1 Samuel 16: 3

For the LORD does not see as man sees; for man looks at the outward appearance, but the LORD looks at the heart."

I was being strengthened and challenged to begin to dig into my own creativity and gifts. Seeking God for revelation and understanding of the meaning of value from God's perspective. First, I realized according to Genesis 1:27 the very fact that we were made by the hand of the creator in his very image.

I had come to a revelation, during my deep processing, that what I consider value was not valued at all. It was judged by the rules of men and not God my creator. Living in a world where value is determined by how you look, how much money or material items you have, or by your status and power. My mind was in a state of great transition. I had begun to understand and embrace new thinking while allowing old thinking to be uprooted. Value began to be so much clearer when I began to embrace how much God loved and value me. My prayer was, "God, show me through Your lenses how you see me. Not the lies I was told or the false perceptions I have received." I ask God to show me my beauty and he did.

Jeremiah 31:3

"Yes, I have loved you with an everlasting love; therefore with"

This began to change my life and help me to embrace my real value according to God. I had been so lost but now I was truly ABLE to see. I start feeling good and the process I had gone through, to get to this point, was great and also necessary. God's great love for me guided me through the dark places and nights. He allowed me to began to understand my value which helped me to stop making certain decisions and helped me to understand what and why I did some of the things I had been doing.

The biggest things I had to face is why I wanted love, desired to be accepted, and receive value from others. I needed to understand how to value me, love me, accept me, embrace me, and all that God created me to be with all the flaws, mistakes, and failures; the low-value moments as well as the high mountain experiences.

Jeremiah 31:3

The LORD hath appeared of old unto me, saying, Yea, I have loved thee with an everlasting love: therefore with lovingkindness
have I drawn thee.

Understanding my value caused me to be drawn away from the world. Each day I was being drawn in closer to God. I was now learning to let somethings and people go because it was not good for my own mental state. I was getting this deep understanding to value my state of mind and well-being that I did not allow people, situations, or even past mistakes put me in a place where I felt undervalued. I realized that that was something that I had to start within me.

I was in search and because I was in deep search of God's view of me this changed my life. I found that through many trials and things I faced I have always been valued by God. But I did not allow myself to see it. I had made so many mistakes I questioned how was I going to be of any value to anyone including myself. How was I going to help anyone if I could not understand my value in God?

"When Diamonds are found they are in a dark place. As I researched information on Diamonds, I learned that creation begins 100 miles underground where tremendous heat and pressure crystallize carbon into rough Diamonds. Diamonds then reach the surface through a specific kind of volcanic eruption, called a kimberlite eruption. I then looked up the Kimberlite eruption. It is a small but powerful volcanic eruption."

After reading this, I had a powerful revelation. With so much pressure and coming from a dark yet powerful eruption, the Diamond is of great value but not at first. It goes through a tedious process before the value is able to be seen or known. Just like a lot of us we go through various stages where there is cutting and breaking only to make us who God has called us to be. Without these various stages, we would not understand nor appreciate our value. My own life stages have allowed me to understand my value. I can no longer say I am a Diamond in the rough. I now say I am a Diamond out of the rough. I remember where I come from but my focus is now on where I am going.

I no longer hold my head down. I no longer allow the shame to try and choke me out. I no longer think I am not worthy of being happy and living life. One day, I just stood in the mirror, looked at myself, and said, "I am crafted by the Father's I am made in the image of God." Who am I to say to God I do not like myself when I was created in God's image and his likeness? I encourage you to take your own journey. Take the time to know and understand how valuable you are to God. It is a process you will not regret.

I thank God for who I have become today. and the woman I am continuing to evolving into God-ordained. My new fresh outlook on life has changed drastically. I now understand my purpose, now I can help others. It's not about making a statement to the world saying, "I know my value." It's about living life in such a way that you know without saying a word. I want you to choose today your value in God, not the world's systems.

We can value one another when we value ourselves. The streets that I came from showed no love. I had to build a tough exterior but my heart was far from it. I made decisions that affect my well being. I was hurting myself not only by doing things physically but also mentally. There came a time when I asked myself this question, "How long am I going to allow the damage and self destruction continue?" It was like waking up from a deep sleep but now I have come to a great awareness. My answer came by way of actions. I began to subtract anything that was not adding to me. My peace, joy, happiness, and metal wellness became a priority.

I looked and desire to be validated by others. Years of suffering in silence. I just wanting to be free of what people thought of me. Would they accept me how they viewed me? It took many years for that to break off of me. Many layers and years of unhealthy thinking about myself and if others would accept me. Though these places were rooted in wanting acceptance from those who I considered to be important people, the fact of the matter is it hurt very much.

I was also dealing with so much rejection it held me in a place of not speaking up or voicing myself because of the fear that I would lose someone's validation or lose the person completely. Yes, I made bad mistakes due to the root of my problem and not dealing with my issues. But I learned to just live and keep going on while I had wide-open wounds. This is where the value of who God ordained me to be broke the chains of these negative thoughts and perceptions.

The light had broken through and I was able to walk away from shame and rejection. I learned to appreciate my own voice. I came to know that my voice matters. I came to know that I had been validated and accepted by God. And that validations surpass any person's valuations. I see a new me now. I can move into the polishing. I'm being presented as a ready vessel to walk in my purpose by walking away from fear, rejection, and low self-esteem. Now for the polishing process. There are no borders or walls when it comes to the treasure that lies within.

PRAYER

God,

I thank you that you have made after Your imagine that I am; fearfully and wonderfully made. Lord forgive me for thinking less of myself in the past and help me to understand and embrace the treasure. You have placed within me. Give me an understanding of my value and most importantly how much you love me. I decree I will began to speak and think differently about myself and move forward in my destiny. Amen.

Reflection: Take a moment to reflect on what you have just read. In this time take a moment to understand who God has called you to be and the great value of your purpose.

PRINCIPLES TO UNDERSTAND YOUR VALUE

💎 Understand who you are so that you will understand your value.

💎 Take steps to dig into knowing and understanding your God-given purpose in life.

💎 Transform your thoughts and words to speak life over my life.

💎 Invest in self-care and self wellness; physically, emotionally, and mentally.

💎 How has what you learned effective you and those around you.

Chapter 4

POLISHING

ISAIAH 61: 3

To appoint unto them that mourn in Zion, to give unto them beauty for ashes, the oil of joy for mourning, the garment of praise for the spirit of heaviness; that they might be called trees of righteousness, the planting of the LORD, that he might be glorified.

During my time of reaching the process of a Diamond, I realized that my life was parallel to the steps of processing. All the things that I have had to go through lead up to this point. I realize that all things have a purpose and with this not only will things be revealed but it will also be manifested. After my own internal battles in my mind and my heart, I thank God for every moment because of this I have a greater appreciation of life, an authentic place of becoming humble, and a place where I embrace the women that God has preordained for me to be. I pray that you embrace this place.

I can now say that I am at peace. There are many people that contribute to my polishing. These people played a key role in the development of my self-awareness, my self struggles strengths, and weaknesses. God allowed me to cross paths with these wonderful people who did not realize the great impact that they had on my life. I was able to own and take responsibility for some of the things that had done. Once I was able to do this, I became free; no more condemnation. I was free and my focus was now on the future and how I could effectively help those I come in contact with. I can help others. Understand that you too can shine bright like a Diamond.

I began to dig deep, reaching out, and moving beyond my place of comfort into a place of how can I help change shape, and impact the lives of others who felt that all hope was gone. The process of the polishing is not only to make sure that I am polished but how can I help others. I began to move beyond a place of thinking of myself. I began to think of how my personal testimony could help others. I began to have compassion for those I came in contact with. I began to understand that this is a team effort and that I did not make it to this point alone but with the help of many that walked alongside me to ensure that I would make it.

The polishing has allowed me to become focused and driven in a way that I had never thought I could be. Now, the love I was so desperate for I no longer yearn for from people. The dark places and things I had gone through made me wise and stronger. The bad decision I made I felt no more condemnation about. This drove me to make sure that all that God had placed in my earthly vessel will be given into my life journey of helping others while in return fulfilling my purpose. Purpose be intentionally about it work hard on it and never give up.

Now that I am this beautiful Diamond, I have an appreciation of what one must go through to obtain such beauty luster, and shine. In order for me to understand the price, I had to go through the cutting. To understand my value as a human being, I had to go through digging to understanding the value of who God created me to be. I had to face some dark things but deliverance came so that I could shine bright like a Diamond. Embracing the dark in order to understand the light

Even now I am on a forever road of processing as I am forever learning and forever always remaining teachable in ways of how I can become better. I will continue to evolve into what God has placed in me. Even though I am not in certain places and my mindset has changed, there is always room for improvement. Always a place to continue to receive knowledge always obtaining wisdom. We never stop growing as long as we are here and know we have a purpose in God. I challenge myself daily to create and be productive, how can I improve and do better? Not just for the purpose of self but the purpose of helping others.

Sometimes I just take moments to reflect on my life, where God has brought me from, and how my mindset has evolved and the old way I used to think have been left behind. I now take time to celebrate even the small successes and victories. There used to be a time where I would be in a place of condemnation or always asking the questions of why or what if's. I now have beauty for ashes. Even though I was found in a dark place, hidden from clear view, and had dirt all over me I realize that it was necessary. The light brought exposure to my darkness. But yet I have always been a Diamond I was lost. But now I am polished which was brought about because of my dark place experience.

I came to the understanding that being in the dark is not always a bad thing. We sometimes relate darkness to something negative. But I begin to receive a profound revelation that my dark place was not all bad actually being in the dark I was being cultivated prepared and developed for my purpose; a place where I was being prepared to shine after I had been cut gone through the process. I had to be refined realigned with

36

my God-given mandate.

ARE YOU WILLING TO EMBRACE
EVEN THE DARK PLACE?

I would have never thought that the dark place that brought me so much pain would be used to develop and shape me into the Diamond I have become. Once a hopeless girl, now I have developed into a mature woman. Everything was necessary, nothing was wasted. I have been polished, been through the fire, and destined to shine bright like a Diamond. I will forever continue my process. I will forever be on this journey. Even now, there are times I may need to be cut. This ensures that I will not get compliance but continue to release all that God has placed within being on the potters will we must be pliable

" The polish of the Diamond is the shine that is given to a Diamond after it is cut. Polishing a Diamond allows light to reflect off its surface, giving it that beautiful shine. After a stone is cut, polishing refines the look of the stone to give it a flawless finish. "

REFLECTION: Take a moment to reflect on your polishing process, what have you learned and what wisdom you have gained.

PRAYER

Dear God,

    I embrace and thank you for my polishing process in my life through all my mistakes shortcomings and challenges. Thank you for giving me an understanding of my process and even my dark places that have to lead up to and developed me in my polishing. Now, I like to celebrate every obstacle that God you helped me to overcome. I thank you, God, for the new and transformed mind, new places, new experiences, and newfound hope that I embrace now. I have been polished and I am now ready to step into my new place. Old things have passed away and I thank you for the new. Amen

PRINCIPLES FOR POLISHING

💎 How has your process helped you in being polished.

💎 Now that you have been polished what steps will you take to uphold your shine and luster.

💎 How can you shine help in the development of those who you have been called to.

💎 In what ways will you acknowledge and celebrate your success and progress that you have made.

💎 Staying connected to others who can enhance and develop you on your way.

Chapter 5

DIGGING DEEP

Jeremiah 29:11

For I know the thoughts that I think toward you, says the LORD, thoughts of peace and not of evil, to give you a future and a hope.

As I stated before, "the process of Diamond creation begins 100 miles underground where tremendous heat and pressure crystallize carbon into rough Diamonds". I read this and I began to think of my own digging. I also began to think about God. He dug and dug for me and found me, even though I was covered by dirt and deep into sin. God began to deal with me on how he dug for me. We should dig for those who are also covered in dirt and a deep place. Are we willing to dig for another who may be too weak to dig for themselves?

The desires of my heart began to change. I had developed a deep compassion to help pull those from a dark place. I came to a profound revelation that God allowed me to be covered so I would know and understand God's mercy and grace. Now IS the time after the shinning to help others overcome. So, you ask, how can I dig deeper? What more could there be? To answer those questions, you have gone through a process of cutting and now it is time for you to dig deep for the treasure.

1 Corinthians 4:7

But we have this treasure in earthen vessels, that the excellency of the power may be of God, and not of us.

God has placed a treasure deep down within you. You were predestined for greatness and such should and will come forth as you are digging deep. Do all you can and allow God to stretch you. Your purpose is bigger than just you. This purpose helps those whom God has called to you to.

Dig deep this is so important because there is only one you that God has placed individually inside of each one of us. Thou your you may be different you are so needed. Take the needed time to really dig deep into your purpose. This is the reason for the entire process. This is why we were tried in the fire. Are you afraid of a little dirt? Dirt is necessary for growth

You have to be willing to go the extra mile. At some point, it may seem uncomfortable, sometimes you may not quite understand the process, or even how are you going to get to the hidden treasure. For me, it was a lengthy process. It was not something that will happen overnight. I remember many days of frustration of such a lengthy process my faith was being tried. And yet, I had to keep digging to uncover this treasure that was within me. This hidden component of my Diamond process.

I had many questions for God. What is my purpose? How will I get there? Who will help me? How will this happen? I felt that I had wasted so much time that I did not want to waste anymore. As I started walking out my purpose and these things took place, the treasure began to unfold. The Diamond was be extracted and the value had just gone up.

Sometimes digging deep much will be uncovered. The most valuable things will come forth. The Diamond is found with a deep digging process. Are you willing to dig deep even when you are tired and discouraged? Do you know that God strengthens us all to dig deep? God is pushing us to go after this treasure that was placed on the inside of us.

As I continued to seek God, he would reveal more when I let go of my past, personal failures, and my own way. That is when I received a great revelation. The digging was worth it and the treasure from within was unfolding. As you continue to dig and let go, you will know and understand your original intent for which you were sent into the earth.

I pray that as you are in your digging process you would be open to the new things God wants to do with you, you would embrace what and who God has called you to be, and your mind is renewed with a fresh perspective of your true purpose and the great revelation of the great treasure that lies within. Know that this treasure is worth digging for. This is what God has placed in you and your assignment in the earth realm. It's a great uncovering. That uncovering is what God has placed within you. May you embrace, move forward, and push past any obstacles that would try to come your way.

The willingness to dig to uncover and unveil who you have been called to be can stretch. As you are in your place of uncovering, you will come upon some of the greatest things regarding yourself and your value. There is a purpose and yet so much more to uncover.

During my discovery, I began to embark upon a new way of thinking and seeing myself. I am still uncovering all of who I am; my gifts, talents, creativity, purpose, and destiny. I must say it has been an interesting journey so far. I know there is so much more, the same is for you. Take a moment and reflect on your digging process how you feel and what you have discovered. Write down your thoughts because it will help.

PRAYER

Dear God,

I pray that as I embrace my digging process to unveil and reveal the treasure and self-discovery of my value. I pray that I would be patient with the process. Help me to see and understand who I am and what I have been called to. Help me to take focus on the things that matter and not be distracted by the things of my past. I put away all shame and condemnation that would try to keep me bound. Open my mind and transform my thoughts so that I can take and understand this new perspective towards my own life journey and releasing of my treasure while I am digging. May this treasure not only help me but help those who you have called me to. Amen.

PRINCIPLES FOR DIGGING

◆ Be willing to take the necessary steps to dig for your treasure and know that you are worth it..

◆ Be patient with yourself. Allow time to help you unveil and reveal who you are.

◆ Accept what has been shown to you during your digging process. This may include some pros and cons.

◆ Make sure you are connected with people who will push and hold you accountable.

◆ Being uncomfortable is a part of the process. Make times for reflection and prayer.

◆ Stay focus. Don't allow anything to distract you from your digging process. This includes old mindsets, old ways of thinking, and past relationships that were not healthy or even family building a prayer life. And receiving wise council is important

◆ Digging can be a tiring process. Make sure to take moments to refresh and renew your mind and spirit.

◆ Be determined to keep digging until God reveals your assignment as your treasure is being released.

Chapter 6

MAINTAINING YOUR SHINE

Matthew 5:16

Let your light so shine before men, that they may see your good works,

and glorify your Father which is in heaven.

Do you know that even after a Diamond has become a place of beauty and shine there is still some upkeep that must be done? The Diamond can lose the full capacity of shine or become dull looking. It's still a Diamond but it must be cleaned often to keep shinning at its full capacity.

"Diamond jewelry worn on the body will attract dirt from the environment and from your body." In my Diamond process, I had to learn that I would not allow any unnecessary dirt to get on me. No one was going to keep kicking dirt on me. I had come to know and understand who I am and to which I belong. But I also knew that dirt is necessary for growth. So the dirt was not all bad.

This is in comparison with our own life. We to attract dirt. Not just to our bodies but to our spirits as well. This causes cloudiness in our seeing and produces a burled view. After I had come to my place of shining, I had to realize there were some things I had/ have to do to maintain my shine. For me, I have to clean my mind daily. It needed to be renewed even though I had been covered and processed understanding my treasure yet there was still more understanding I needed.

I had not arrived. I am forever a student when it comes to Holy Spirit speaking to me. I realized that some dirt just happens but some dirt I allowed. I now needed to become responsible for what I allowed and own it. This is definitely a process. I had to recognize the things that were dimming my shine. I had to get rid of these things so that my shine would remain. I also realize that in this life some dirt and dust cannot be avoided.

My thinking had to be filtered daily by writing down my thoughts. I reflected on what happened to me daily, weekly, and yearly. I had to take introspect on my own maintenance. I had to realize that maintaining my shine was also to make sure that I was moving in my purpose. I realized being nonproductive is not an option. You know when things stand still they have the capacity to collect more dust.

"Diamonds are natural magnets for grease, so they're not easy to keep clean. When a Diamond is handled, the oils from your fingers adhere to the Diamond's surface and affect its brilliance and fire". Living in such a world where there is so much going on, we are all going to attract some dirt. But it is up to us to make sure we take the necessary steps in cleaning and maintaining our shine.

I could remember there was a point, after digging for my treasure in the discovery of myself and understanding my value, I had to also deal with a true mind shift. I had come to realize that this is not a process. In order to maintain this beauty, I had to understand the cleaning. In some ways, old thoughts and perception would cross my mind along with old ways of doing and seeing things. I began to notice repeating cycles that were effecting my growth and development.

At times my thoughts would be cloudy and it was hard to see. I began to see, along the way, that these things caused me to attract dirt and dim my shine. I had to use the Word of God and prayer as well as setting up principles in helping me to maintain my shine. I realized that having a little dirt on you is not all bad. It allows times of self-reflection and helps in our growth. Just like a flower, it needs to be planted in dirt so it can grow. The seed develops in a dark place and then its spots above the dirt. There you can see the beauty. So, a little dirt will not hurt. It's all apart of being developed. Take the time to look and discover that dirt. It reveals to us there is a cleaning that must take place. Dirt also helps us grow and develop.

Take a moment and reflect on how and what you have allowed to dim your shine. What has caused you to allow dirt to be thrown upon you? For me, some dirt was given permission to stick to me because of my mindset, what I had been through because of wanting to be accepted and valued by others. And then, it was the dirt or dust that just happen because of life. It's kinda like walking in the rain and people are driving by in their cars. They drive through a puddle of water and the water splash upon you. You could not help that one. You just happen to be walking at that time.

These are times I took in-depth evaluations of myself. During these evaluations, I noticed that not only the dust and the dirt that dimmed me but also what I allowed. I learned how to set boundaries so that my shine will not be dimmed by what I allow. The Holy Spirit helped me come up with a plan of action to maintain my shine. Maintaining our shine is not all about us. It is about the Glory of God being revealed through us. Take a moment to reflect and understand the importance of maintaining your shine.

PRAYER

God,

I thank you for all you have allowed to take place in my process of maintaining who you have called me. Thank you for giving me a greater understanding of what I must do to maintain my shine. Let my shine reflect and represent who you are within me. Cleanse me from all unhealthy thoughts, perceptions, vain imaginations, and the voices of negative; thoughts that go through my mind. Cleanse me from the things my ears have heard and my eyes have seen. May my ears be inclined to hear Your voice and not be influenced by the words and deeds of people who are not guided by Holy Spirit. Help me in these moments of spiritual maintenance develop and reflect on my own ways that will dim the shine. I pray according to Your Word. Amen.

PRINCIPLES FOR MAINTAINING YOUR SHINE

💎 Take time to understand the purpose of maintaining your shine.

💎 Renew your mind daily. It will help you maintain your shine.

💎 Take time to yourself to reflect often. Unload, release, and let go of anything that would try to dim your light.

💎 Remember that you are unique. Don't allow anyone to dim your light just because they do not understand their own.

💎 Find ways to invest in your self-development.

💎 Always remember, Our paths must point back to Christ. Your shine is what God has given to you so don't allow it to be taken away.

Chapter 7

THE FINISH WORK

2 Corinthians 8:11

but now you also must complete the doing of it; that as there was a readiness to desire it, so there also may be a completion out of what you have.

I must say that we are not truly finished. It's just certain things have finishing points in our lives. Once one thing is complete, we move on to another. Regarding my own journey, I must say it has been a bit of a challenge but in those challenges of the completion, it made me better. I pressed more, dug more, and push past all and every limitation that tried to keep me bound. Not just those of life but that of my own thoughts, ways, and actions.

There used to be such a challenge for me to finish. But I received a great revelation, why go through the entire process only to get to the finish line and give up. That makes no sense. At times, we do not see how far we have come and how close we are to the finish. I started making little small goals to finish. After some time, I became more detailed and planned on finishing what good had started within me.

Philippians 1:6

being confident of this very thing, that He who has begun a good work in you will complete it until the day of Jesus Christ;

I realized that I could not be confident in my own strength but confident in God's strength that he had placed within me. I would be able to finish the work that was set before me and that there will be a work that needs to be finished until the coming of Christ. This was a major turning point in my life. I began to understand the start is just as important as the finish. After finishing one thing after another, the small things, I was able to move forward in the bigger things. I learned to celebrate the small success. Even though I made mistakes along the way, I learned from them.

I was able to understand that my finishing was not all about me but helping others. I realized , completing what I was called to ensure forward movement in helping others. Imagine doing all the work to dig for Diamonds, go through the cutting process, shape the Diamond to all of a sudden stop. Every step is vital for the development of the Diamond. We would not be able to enjoy the splendor the beauty and understand the true value.

Finishing work ensures that I am becoming. I am evolving every time I finish what God has assigned me to. I realized that each time I would finish it would be different. Some assignments may come with ease and some required more of a push or it was a bit more challenging.

As you face your finished work, be encouraged, and know that so much will come forth that will impact your life and those who are connected to you. Be confident in who

God created you to be. If you need to start small and don't compare your journey with anyone else's. We all have a journey but in many ways it is different.

How do you look at your journey and your finished work? Sometimes we need to slow down reflect and see what we have learned. Don't move forward before completing what you have started This is very important finishing insures that as you move forward you have what you need to continue on to what is next. Sometimes we want to move forward yet we leave things incomplete with no results when we finish we are reaping results which helps in development and builds us in character . Making sure we align ourselves with hearing from Holy Spirit. Somethings we have not been called to and sometimes it could just be the timing. The will and purpose of our treasure that God has placed on the inside of us is not to just sit on it. Not only to start it but finished and finish strong. The beauty of God and His grace and power.

We have come to a place where we have finished somethings but there is more before us. How will we embrace the things that you have accomplished. I had to learn to celebrate the little victories in private. I had to acknowledge my growth and development even if it was little. But I realize that little things can make a major impact. I pray that you would be endowed with the grace to finish what you have stated. I must say I am so grateful for this journey that I am having now. My past helped me to impact my today. It taught me much, revealed my weaknesses, and exposed my shortcomings. Not to condemn but to correct errors in thinking. These areas hinder me from moving forward and with no forward movement, I had been unsuccessful in being able to finish strong. With a transformed mind, different outlook, and adjustment of my lenses from which I look through I have been able to move forward and finish those things in which God had given for me to do.

Somethings were not finished. I had to go back with a fresh new perception and complete my assignment. You may be asking, why go back to finish? I needed to align correctly. When I say this, I'm not saying I go back to old things but I set in order what God has placed me to do. I did know and understand that some things were not to be picked up because it was not my assignment. I like for you to take a moment to reflect on your own process of finished work. What does that look like to you?

PRINCIPLES FOR THE FINISH WORKED

- 💎 Be open to learn what it will take to finish.
- 💎 Have a finish line mentality.
- 💎 Invest into your own self-advancement. Be willing to put in the work.
- 💎 Be in touch with how you feel regarding your finishing. No time to keep looking in the past.; moving forward requires a forward view mentality.Be in expectation of what you are expecting of results what results are you wanting to see.
- 💎 Be okay if things do not go as plan, you may require a reroute or a reboot.

We learn every day that we must allow ourselves to hear the Holy Spirit and rid ourselves of the negative thoughts and voices. Going before God allows us to hear and also gain strategy and wisdom which gives us an understanding on how to apply this to our lives.

Proverbs 16:3

Commit your works to the LORD, And your

thoughts will be established.

God is the greatest strategist. The creator, the one that places the treasure on the inside of all of us. Be intentional about your finish work, dig deep, and pull out what you need. Because all we need to finish God has placed on the inside of us. He wouldn't have give us the assignment without the tools to be able to finish.

The finished work of a Diamond is great we get to enjoy all of its beauty and shine because another man finished the work. No finish. No manifestation. No growth. No progress. No effect. No lives being changed or reformed of those whom God has called us to. Let us own our finish. Yet, we know with life things happen. But we must press and with the pressing, the anointing will come forward, your gifts will manifest, and life will change.

PRAYER

God,

I thank you for all you have placed within me. I ask for wisdom on how I can apply this to my life and how I can finish strong. I decree that I will tap into what you have placed on the inside of me. I ask that you would download strategies and knowledge on how I can finish strong. Connect me with people that will help cultivate, challenge, and extract the best out of me so that I can finish everything you have given me. I will not accept defeat. I will not procrastinate. I decree I will level up and own what you have given me to finish. I repent for things that I have not finished. I move forward in confidence knowing that you have begun a good work in me and I will finish strong. Amen.

Bonus Chapter

DECLARATIONS

There is power in the words that we speak in the atmosphere. That's why it is so important that we know and understand what we are speaking. Words are powerful enough to shape our atmosphere and change our lives.

Job 22:28

You will also declare a thing, And it will be established for you;

So light will shine on your ways.

TODAY AND OFTEN MAKE THESE DECLARATIONS OVER YOUR LIFE:

- I decree and declare I am blessed with all things concerning me and my life.
- I decree that success, favor, abundance, and grace follow me everywhere I go.
- I decree and declare I am walking in confidence and wisdom given to me by

God.

- 💎 I decree I am moving forward in my God-ordained assignment and I will see manifestations in the earth.
- 💎 I decree and declare I am loaded daily with benefits from God.
- 💎 I decree and declare I am made in the image of God.
- 💎 I decree I walk by faith and I am loaded every day with God's Word in my heart.
- 💎 I decree and declare I am a finisher.
- 💎 I decree and declare that I am victorious in Christ Jesus.
- 💎 I decree and declare that the works of my hands prosper.
- 💎 I decree and declare I am in good health, my body, and mind are healthy.
- 💎 I decree and declare I am the head and not the tail.
- 💎 I decree and declare nothing will be wasted all will be used to glorify God.
- 💎 I decree and declare I will not allow negatives words from my mouth or the words of others to take me off the focus of my assignment.
- 💎 I decree and declare I am seated in heavenly places with Christ Jesus far above powers and principalities.
- 💎 I decree and declare I am a son of God.
- 💎 I decree and declare I am a child of God.
- 💎 I decree and declare I am an ambassador of the Kingdom of God.
- 💎 I decree and declare that I have forgiven myself and others.
- 💎 I decree and declare I will no longer live in shame and guilt.
- 💎 That old things have passed away and that God has made me new.

❖ I decree and declare that even in my dark places, trails, and tribulations I will be strengthened by Holy Spirit.

❖ I decree and declare I am a good steward over all that God has given me.

❖ I decree and declare I will reflect on all that God has shown me.

❖ I decree and declare that I will impact the lives of those who are connected to me in a positive way.

❖ I decree and declare that I am loaded daily with God's Word and prayer.

❖ I decree that I am unique and I embrace my individuality.

❖ I decree and declare all that God has for me I shall and will obtain.

When you declare these things declare them in confidence knowing they will produce results in your atmosphere. Do not look at the current circumstances and do not allow unbelief, fear, or doubt to stop you. These declarations are providing an atmosphere to produce manifestation and much results. Activate your faith to know that what you are declaring will and shall come to pass. Follow God's principles in His Word. Stay focused and know that God's plan is working together for your good.

"Processed by God been through the fire destine to shine bright like a Diamond"

~Hope T. Melton

Author's Notes

I thank you for joining me on part of my journey as I shared I hope that this has encouraged edify and lifted you. I pray that what I have shared will help to encourage you to keep moving forward. Being able to share with you is an honor as we share with one another we all will become victorious and over comers you were born to shine. Allow the light of who you were created to be shine so bright. You are a Diamond no matter what you have had to face in life no matter how different we all my be we all share one thing. We all have purpose and destiny.

My journey is not yet finished I have much more to share.
To Be Continued...

THE MAKING
OF A
DIAMOND

My Personal Journey

Hope T. Melton

NOTES

blog.brilliance.com (2020). How to shop for Diamond engagement rings. Retrieve from https://blog.brilliance.com/

britannica.com (2020). Kimberlite eruption. Retrieve from https://www.britannica.com/science/kimberlite-eruption

brittanysfinejewelry.com (2020). The Diamond process: from deep underground to your favorite ring. Retrieve from https://brittanysfinejewelry.com/Diamond-process-deep-underground-favorite-ring/

captetowndiamandmuseum.org. (2020). Museums in Cape Town. Retrieve from https://www.capetownDiamondmuseum.org/

datlasestates.com. (2020). How to take care of your Diamond. Retrieve from https://datlasestates.com/where-to-sell-Diamond-ring

en.wikipedia.com. (2020). Diamond cutting. Retrieve from https://en.wikipedia.org/wiki/Diamond_cutting

forbes.com. (2020). The Origin Of Geological Terms: Diamonds. Retrieve from https://www.forbes.com/sites/davidbressan/2016/04/30/the-origin-of-geological-terms-Diamonds/

leibish.com (2020). The Diamond cleaning guide. Retrieve from https://www.leibish.com/the-Diamond-cleaning-guide-article-419#:~:text=Diamond%20jewelry%20worn%20on%20the,is%20worn%20on%20the%20hand

withclarity.com (2020). Diamond polish. Retrieve from https://www.withclarity.com/education/Diamond-education/Diamond-polish

Made in the USA
Columbia, SC
13 June 2024

36922297R00037